Contents

Safety First

You don't need to wrap your children in cotton wool to keep them safe, but with a little bit of forward planning you can help to reduce the number of needless accidents that happen every year.

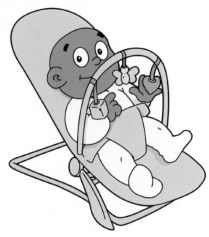

Babies depend on you entirely for their safety and it's surprising how quickly they learn to move.

- Always use a five-point harness in buggies, baby seats and car seats.

- Never leave babies on a changing table, bed or sofa.

- Don't put bouncing cradles or baby car seats on tables or work surfaces.

- Never shake your baby.

Babies and toddlers do not automatically know what is dangerous, so it is really important that you:

- Always watch them.

- Remove them from danger.

- Explain about safety from an early age.

- Make your home safer for little ones.

Safety First

Children become more independent as they grow and learn about the world around them, but they still depend upon you to keep them safe.

- Make them aware of dangers.

- Explain why, don't just say, 'NO - don't do that!'

- Show them how to do things safely.

- Keep reminding them about safety.

Have you looked both ways? Is it safe to cross?

And remember:

- Shouting or smacking will **NOT** teach children about safety.

- Children love to copy, so set a good example.

Celebration Time

Before special events and outings:

- Discuss possible dangers and safety precautions with your children.

- Make sure that you know who is responsible for younger children.

Have fun safely

You must stay with me, because fireworks can burn you very badly if you are too close.

Reduce the Risk at Home

Making your Home Safer

Children are curious by nature. They will usually go exploring and try to make sense of the objects they find by touching, smelling and tasting them. From small and sharp objects to large pots and pans, children will try to learn about every household item and appliance they see. This means it's time to start making your home safer for your children.

First Things First

Get down on your hands and knees and have a crawl around your house. You may feel a little silly but by seeing your home from your toddler's position you'll be able to see what they can see and, more importantly, what they can reach for.

Move anything that you think could cause a risk to your child's safety.

Pay particular attention to hanging wires and cables, plug sockets and fireplaces.

Reduce the Risk at Home

Staying Safe

You can't be everywhere at once, but there are things you can do to help your children stay safe when you are not there.

Don't put that in your mouth, you might swallow it and choke!

- Teach your children about dangers and explain to them why they must not do certain things.

- Teach children not to touch things that they are unsure about.

- Monitor progress; don't give too much freedom too soon. They may need reminding many times before they learn.

- Use child safety equipment wherever possible.

- Don't forget your children will copy you, think about the example you are setting.

- Take care when visiting other people's homes where child safety may not have been considered.

So that's how she gets her hair straight!!

Fire Safety

Fires in the home

Fires in the home cost lives every year, but there are many simple steps that you can take to reduce the risk.

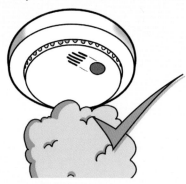

- Install smoke alarms on every floor of your home, test them every week to check that they are working.

- Keep matches, lighters and cigarettes out of sight and reach of young children.

- Always put out cigarettes properly.

- Always use a fireguard.

- Don't dry clothes near a fire, over a fireguard, in the oven or in the microwave.

- Fire retardant does NOT mean that it won't burn.

- Don't overload sockets, use one plug per socket or a bank.

- Plan how your family will escape if a fire breaks out.

Fire Safety

Deep Fat Frying

It's better to use a thermostat controlled deep fat fryer, because it can't overheat. If you must deep fry in a pan always remember:

- Never fill the pan more than a third full of oil.

- If the oil is smoking it's too hot, let it cool before cooking.

- Never leave the pan unattended.

- If it does catch fire - don't take risks. Turn off the heat if it is safe to do so. **GET OUT, STAY OUT** and call **999**.

- NEVER throw water over it.

Candles

Candles are a popular feature in modern homes, but they can be very dangerous if left unattended or not used carefully.

- Always put candles in a proper holder on a steady surface away from curtains and out of reach of children and pets.

- Take care with tea-lights that get hot enough to melt plastic surfaces such as TV tops and baths.

- Extinguish candles completely when you leave a room.

Burns and Scalds

The vast majority of burn injuries to children happen in their own home, but most of these burns can be prevented.

- Never pass hot drinks over babies' heads or drink tea or coffee whilst holding a baby or young child.

  Hot drinks can still scald young children up to 15 minutes after they have been made.

- Use a bottle warmer or jug of hot water to heat milk and shake well. Microwaves cause hot spots that can scald a baby's mouth.

- Use a kettle with a curly flex and keep it well back from the edge of the worktop.

- Turn saucepan handles towards the back of the cooker and use the back rings if possible.

- Always use fireguards and keep children away from hot appliances.

Burns and Scalds

- Avoid ironing when small children are about.
Store the iron carefully after use.

  Remember even an iron that is turned off can cause serious burns if it has not cooled down.

- Don't let children make hot drinks before they are tall enough to pour from the kettle **without** standing on a chair or having to reach up.

- Always put cold water in the bath first and add hot water after. Check the bath water with your elbow before bathing your child.

- Keep hot hair straighteners out of reach of small children. Never leave them to cool on a bedside cabinet or door handle. Always unplug after use.

Cleaners, Pills and Potions

Accidental poisoning!

The main causes of accidental poisoning are from mistaking cleaning products and medicines for sweets and drinks.

● Keep all medicines and cleaners in a locked cupboard out of reach of small children.

● Buy products that have child resistant caps. Remember child resistant does **NOT** mean child proof.

● Don't coax children to take medicine by suggesting it is a sweet.

They'll make you feel better and they taste like liquorice!

Kid Premiership Cold & Flu Relief
To relieve the symptoms of colds and flu including headaches, sore throats, blocked up nose and fever.

Contains Paracetamol
Do not exceed the stated dose. Do not take with other paracetamol-containing medicines. Immediate medical advice should be sought in the event of an overdose, even if you feel well.

How to take this medicine:
Dissolve the contents of one sachet in a cup of boiling water.

Adults and children over 12 years: take one sachet every 4 to 6 hours. If needed a max of 4 sachets in 24 hours.

Do not give to children und...

COLD & FLU DRINK

● Read medicine labels and always follow instructions.

● Don't take medicines in front of your children, they may try to copy you.

Cleaners, Pills and Potions

- Alcohol is toxic to children, make sure it is out of their reach.

- Tobacco can be lethal to children. Keep cigarettes out of reach, or better still don't smoke.

- Keep all cleaning products and chemicals out of reach of children and in their original containers.

- Don't store chemicals in food cupboards.

- Make sure that you don't have any poisonous plants or berries in the garden.

- Think about where you store garden chemicals. Always keep them in their original containers and out of the reach of children.

Water Safety

- Children can drown in just a few centimetres of water.

- Never leave a child unattended in the bath or paddling pool, not even for a minute.

- Older siblings should not be responsible for younger children in or near water.

- Water is an excellent conductor. Keep all electrical appliances well away from water to avoid electrocution.

- Don't touch electrical appliances with wet hands.

- Mop spills up straight away to avoid slips and falls.

TEACH YOUR CHILD TO SWIM.

Water Safety

- Never leave your child to wander off near water.

- Lakes, canals and rivers are always cold, even in hot weather. The safest way to enjoy them is on an organised trip with professional supervision.

- There can be many dangers lurking beneath the water. Even the best swimmers can be dragged under by currents or get into difficulties.

Air Safety

CIGARETTES ARE EXTREMELY TOXIC TO BOTH YOU AND THE PEOPLE AROUND YOU

There are over 4000 toxic chemicals in cigarette smoke, 69 of which can cause cancer. These chemicals can damage almost every organ in the body.

Toxic ingredients in cigarettes include:
- Nicotine
- Carbon Monoxide
- Acetone
- Arsenic
- Lead
- Turpentine

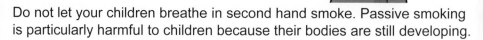

Do not let your children breathe in second hand smoke. Passive smoking is particularly harmful to children because their bodies are still developing.

KEEP YOUR HOUSE AND CAR SMOKE FREE

Smoking during pregnancy is linked to:
- Miscarriage
- Breathing problems
- Stillbirths
- Premature births
- Slow foetus growth
- Cot death
- Weak, poorly babies

For free help and advice on how to quit call **0800 022 4 332** visit **www.smokefree.nhs.uk** or see your GP

What to do if you smell gas

Call Transco, the gas emergency service immediately on 0800 111 999.

I can smell gas! Turn the light on so I can see what I'm doing

- Don't smoke or strike matches.
- Don't turn electrical switches on or off.
- Put out naked flames.
- Open doors and windows.
- Keep people away from the area.
- Turn off the meter at the valve.

Carbon Monoxide (CO)

Carbon monoxide is known as a silent killer because you can't hear, see or smell it - but there are ways you can reduce the risk of poisoning:

- Make sure that all gas appliances and flues are installed and serviced every year by a Gas Safe Registered Engineer.
- Don't block ventilation to your appliances.
- Fit an audible carbon monoxide alarm - available from DIY stores.
- Never run cars, motorbikes or lawn mowers in a closed garage.

For free advice call the Gas Safety Advice Line on 0800 300 363

Food Safety

Preparing food

- Wash your hands before preparing or eating food.

- Clean all work surfaces, especially after preparing raw meat.

- Store chilled food correctly.

- Prepare and store raw and ready to eat foods separately.

Cooking food

- Always check that food is piping hot all the way through before serving.

- Don't reheat food more than once.

- Cooking whilst under the influence of alcohol is dangerous.

- Teach children how to use kitchen equipment safely.
  Children should not cook alone until you are confident of their abilities.

Food Safety

Eating food

- Always sit down to eat and don't let children run around with food or sweets.

- Small children should not have whole nuts or hard sweets - they may choke.

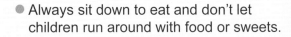

- Never leave little ones to eat or drink alone.

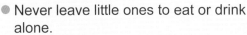

- Use plastic beakers for children, not glass ones.

- Always use a five-point harness for children in highchairs.

- Young children should not use sharp knives.

- Teach children not to eat or drink anything unless given to them by an adult that they can trust.

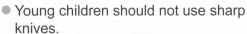

- Be aware of any food allergies and always check the ingredients in new foods.

Safe Play

Safe Play at Home

Take time to think about your home - is it safe for your children?

- Make sure that young children can't open outside doors.
  Keep the keys near the door in case of fire, but out of reach.

- Use safety gates for under twos. Teach older children how to use the stairs safely.

- Don't leave toys where they can be tripped over.

- Small children should not be left alone with pets. Even good-natured animals can be tested when children are around.

- Parental controls should always be set on your internet browser.

- Avoid using baby walkers.

- Don't allow children to play on balconies.

Safe Play

The Lion Mark

The Lion Mark shows that a toy meets British safety standards. Make sure that your children's toys carry this mark to ensure that they are safe.

- Check the age limit on toys before buying them.

- Throw away broken toys.

- Supervise young children with small toys to make sure that they don't put them in their mouths.

- Belts, scarves, ribbons etc are not toys - take care when choosing children's clothing.

- Keep plastic bags out of the reach of young children.

- Older children should not be responsible for babies.

Safe Sleep

Your child depends on you entirely for safety, even whilst sleeping. Think ahead and avoid the dangers.

- Lay your baby down to sleep on his/her back unless your doctor advises otherwise.

- Avoid co-sleeping with your baby.

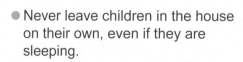

- Never use pillows, duvets or cot bumpers in your baby's cot; they could cause suffocation.

- Never leave children in the house on their own, even if they are sleeping.

- If you go out you must find a responsible adult, whom both you and your child trust, to babysit.

Safe Sleep

- Only use bunk beds for children over 6 years.
  Think about where you put children's beds.
  Fit locks or safety catches to stop windows opening more than 6.5cm.

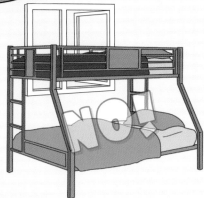

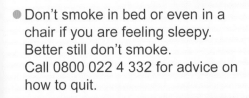

- Avoid dressing your child in pyjamas with ribbons or draw strings and keep beds away from blinds with dangling cords.

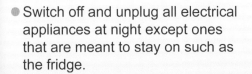

- Don't smoke in bed or even in a chair if you are feeling sleepy.
  Better still don't smoke.
  Call 0800 022 4 332 for advice on how to quit.

- Switch off and unplug all electrical appliances at night except ones that are meant to stay on such as the fridge.

On the Road

- It's not safe for children to play games in the street.

- Shut and bolt the garden gate so that there's no chance of your child running into the street.

- Children under 9 should always have an adult with them to cross the road.

- Don't cross the road whilst on the phone or listening to music.

- BE SAFE, BE SEEN. If you are out in the dark wear something reflective or white so that you can be seen by traffic.

On the Road

Crossing the road safely

Teach children to cross safely.

- Remember to always:
  - Stop
  - Look
  - Listen
  - Think

- Find safe places to cross:
  - Zebra crossing
  - Pedestrian crossing
  - School crossing
  - Bridge or subway

Lead by example:
Don't be careless on the road with your child.
Remember, even babies in pushchairs are learning how to cross the road.

In the Car

- Always wear your seat belt and make sure that children are securely strapped into the car.

- Where possible children should travel in the back seats.

- A child safety seat or booster seat, suitable for a child's size, should be used for all children under 12 years of age or 135cm.

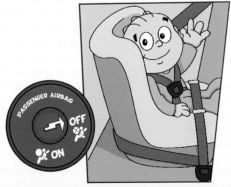

- Never use a rear facing baby seat in the front of the car when the passenger airbag is turned on.

In the Car

- Children should not be left alone in the car.

- Don't use your mobile phone whilst driving.

- Obey speed limits.

- Take care when reversing.

- Store luggage safely in the boot of the car or on a secure roof rack.

Out and About

Some scrapes in the playground are all part of growing up, but it's important to make children aware of safety issues.

- Young children should always be in sight of their adult carer.
Reins will stop toddlers from running into danger, particularly near roads.

- Older children should always tell parents/carers where they are going and agree a time for their return. They should be encouraged to stay with friends and not wander off alone.

- Babies need to be properly strapped into their pram or pushchair.

- Explain to your children why they must not talk to strangers.

- If the sun is shining apply high factor sunscreen at least every 2 hours and make sure that everyone wears a hat.

Babies less than 12 months old should be kept in the shade.